I0087660

All rights reserved. No part of this publication may be reproduced, stored in a retrieval system or transmitted in any form or by any means, electronic, mechanical, photocopying, recording or otherwise, without the written permission of the author.

Text copyright © 2018 Victor Vargas

Content Editing by Betty Hoeffner, Arnie Saks
Final Editing by Dalia Vitkus

Front and Back Cover Design by Betty Hoeffner and Al Baker
Front Cover Photo from Shutterstock
Back Cover Photo by 1014 Photography

Library of Congress Control Number: 2018957893

ISBN-13: 978-0-9759004-4-4

Printed in the United States of America

To buy additional copies of this book email AlmostBulliedToDeath@gmail.com
Quantity discounts are available for bulk purchases

The names of the bullies, gang members and teachers have been changed to protect their identity.

The text messages to Aaron and Derek are real messages.

ALMOST
BULLIED TO
DEATH

BY

VICTOR

VARGAS

Contents

Forward 6

I'm Just a Child 7

First Grade 11

Second Grade 15

School's Out for Summer. 20

Third Grade. 22

Fourth and Fifth Grade 25

The Worst Day of My Life 28

Middle School 33

Initiation 35

Gangs 42

The Bullies Are Back..45

Recruiting 47

Using My Power for Good 49

Rumble? 51

Scholarship Program...53

A Gun and Police at School 54

Leaving the Gang 58

One Last Attack? 60

Summer Break...63

Eighth Grade...65

High School...68

Hope 70

Worldwide TV & Queen Latifah 73

Educating My Haters 74

Community Service..76

Falling in Love...77

Possible Race War...78

Automotive School 80

And Baby Makes Three..82

Hiding Out and Lonely 84

Fatherhood...86

Back to Indiana...88

The Power of Apologizing 89

Today 94

My Music 95

Lessons Learned..96

Acknowledgements / References / Schedule Victor for Book Signing...................98

FORWARD

by

Betty Hoeffner
Co-founder of Hey U.G.L.Y., Author and
Anti-Bullying/Suicide-Prevention Program Developer

When I started reading this book, I could not put it down. It was like watching a movie. Each chapter was a surprise; I could not anticipate how this innocent young boy would next be bullied or threatened. I could think only of the millions of students, counselors, educators and parents who will be helped by Victor Vargas's honest and raw account of what really goes on when no one is looking.

Since 2002 I have dedicated my life to empowering youth to be part of the solution to bullying, substance abuse and suicide. Bullying is a public health issue that is a leading cause of school violence, suicide, substance abuse, self-harm, mental health issues, eating disorders, low grades, truancy and school dropout. It is not, as some say, a 'rite of passage.' We are losing too many youths to suicide due to bullying.

This book should be required reading for educators, school administrators, and youth advocates.

This book needs to be required reading and part of the curriculum for educators, school administrators and youth advocates.

I'M JUST A CHILD

Growing up in the late '90s in a small town in Indiana, I was a happy child in those hot days before first grade. There were no worries to me; bills...ha...what bills? I am a child. Work? Nope not worried; my parents said I was too young to work. Bullies? I knew what it meant, but my parents had taught me to treat people with kindness. So, what was evil going to do to me? Absolutely nothing.

In my early childhood years, I would never have imagined I'd be where I am at today. I grew up with parents who taught me so much. My parents came from Mexico and moved to Sterling, Illinois, where I was born. Mi jefe (father) worked in a tortilla factory where the tortillas were made by hand. Mi jefita (mother) was a stay-at-home mom. They decided to move to La Porte, Indiana when I was six months old for better work. It was an opportune time to leave because gang violence was finding its way into rural western Illinois.

My parents taught me Spanish which was the only language in my house since that was all my parents spoke. *Mi jefita* (my mom) showed me love and taught me about marriage, being faithful to your spouse, and being as one. *Mi jefe* also showed me love, but in a way I didn't understand at such a young age. He played soccer with me on those warm summer days, and those were important bonding times. Seeing how he was always there for my one-year-old sister and me, and how he worked hard to take care of his family, shaped me into who I am today.

The summer right before I was to start first grade, we moved to a neighborhood called Kingsporte in LaPorte. I didn't see any kids in this new neighborhood but, then again, I was shy. Most of the remaining summer days I spent playing soccer by myself outside or helping *mi jefita* with my little sister. I was pleased with my life for the most part.

We lived in the back side of a modular apartment on a dead-end street. We were the first modular apartment on the right as you entered the street. These modulars were typically single level raised buildings containing two apartments with no basement. On the exterior, they had vinyl siding that ended two feet off the ground where it was met by a tin shield perimeter to cover the bare ground. There were gravel spaces on the side, enough to fit two cars. If you drove up too much on the gravel space, you would have been inside the apartment. This dead-end street was so narrow that it only allowed one and a half cars to drive on it.

The inside of the modulars had two bedrooms. Each bedroom had enough room for a queen size bed and a medium-size dresser. In the bedrooms there was at least one wall shared with the modular neighbor.

A few men lived adjacent to us and every weekend they had people over partying, drinking, and yelling. They were los borrachos (the drunks). That summer there wasn't much trouble out of them other than some ruckus that occurred on the weekends. They were very calm as if no one lived there.

A couple of weeks went by and *mi jefita* told me I was going to be starting school. First grade? ARGH#?!!! A frightened look appeared on my face. You know that face you make when you see a ghost or encounter your worst fear. School was something I feared and disliked. Why? I was shy, I didn't have kid friends to hang and play with and my closest cousins lived in California, Illinois, and even Mexico.

I had gone to Lincoln Elementary School in LaPorte for kindergarten where I had made some friends. When I moved, that was the last I saw or heard from them. I feared meeting new kids. Starting all over to make friends seemed difficult mostly because my tongue was different from most, if not all, because I spoke Spanish. My English wasn't very good and neither was my Spanish. I learned English from being a sponge. My brain absorbed the English language mainly from watching cartoons. Jokingly I would tell people I learned English from the Pink Panther or Tom and Jerry. The Pink Panther was a cartoon that literally had a pink panther that didn't talk, but would act silly and crack me up with laughter. Tom and Jerry was a similar cartoon. Tom the cat, and Jerry the mouse, would not speak, yet Jerry made me laugh from always outsmarting Tom. In all actuality, the TV shows that taught me English were Arthur, Barney, Scooby-Doo, and the Looney Tunes.

So, as my nice warm summer days were ending, *mi jefita* would tell me, "*Pronto vamos agarrar tus cosas para la escuela.*" (Soon we are going to get you school supplies.)

I would be disappointed and tell *mi jefita*, "*Si me quieres no me mandas.*" (If you love me you won't send me.) It was silly of me to say something like that, but that is how much I didn't want to go to school. *Mi jefita* loved me no doubt, but she still made me get the school supplies that my soon-to-be teacher asked her to buy. That first day of school kept creeping up on me like dark clouds filled with ice cold rain waiting to fall. That day was unavoidable. *Mi jefita* kept trying to calm me down by telling me I would be making friends. All these words, to a six-year-old who didn't want to go to school, made my summer unpleasant. And I argued about going to school with tiny crystals falling down my face.

FIRST GRADE

August 1998, I was six-years-old and *mi jefita* was walking me to class on my oh-so-big day. *Mi jefe* didn't come with us because he couldn't take the day off from his job at the agricultural supply company.

I inched my feet down the hallway until I made it into Mrs. B's first grade classroom of Handley School. I heard nothing as I walked in, but what I saw was odd. Kids! None of the kids in the class were talking, so I wasn't the only shy kid or maybe they weren't comfortable yet, I thought.

Days went by and my classmates started questioning my ethnicity. I responded the way my parents taught me by saying, "I'm Mexican-American." I thought, that wasn't as bad as I thought it would be, but then my life turned upside down. The kids laughed and said, "American, you ain't no American." Of course, I didn't know why they would say something like that. *Mi jefita* always told me I was Mexican-American. In time I could have gotten over it, but their bullying continued. The bullying boys were dressed in regular blue jeans and nice button up shirts or Polos. My style of clothing was not far from theirs. I wore blue jeans as well with my plain T-shirts because I didn't own any brand name clothing. Most of my wardrobe came from Wal-Mart or K-Mart. I wondered if that was the reason they picked on me.

I never told my parents about the bullying. I would get picked up from school by *mi jefita*, who would always ask, "*Como te fue en la escuela*" (how was school?).

I would quickly tell her all I did that day and never mentioned the hurtful encounters with the other students. You might think I was dumb for not telling my parents, but put your feet in my shoes. Translation was done **by me** for my parents. If my parents went to the school for a meeting with the teacher or principal, it would be **me** doing all of the talking...a six-year-old, in front of an adult, translating all their words filled with a child's emotions. That would make any child scared that they might get in trouble or worse, labeled a tattletale.

For a while, the verbal confrontations stopped. Boy was I relieved, but then it started back up again. The worst was the fact that none of the teachers, or recess supervisors, ever saw the confrontations. There was one time, during a confrontation, when I did tell Mrs. B. about how Cody (one of my classmates) was saying, "You're not from this country you *beaner*." Mrs. B. pulled me and Cody aside. When she asked him if he said that, he replied with a simple, "No," and that was that. I thought the teacher having that talk to us would make the kid stop bullying me. I figured he could tell I was getting tired of hearing it. A week after the two of us were pulled aside, Mrs. T. who was the kid's mother AND a teacher at the school, pulled me aside.

"Now you listen to me," said Mrs. T. "You better stop accusing my son about saying racial things to you."

She said it so rudely I felt like crying because I was having a teacher up in my face making me feel trapped in a corner. After that I tried my hardest to avoid those boys until the school year ended.

I couldn't have been more excited to have that year end. My English had improved slightly and I had kept to myself. That summer was better; kids moved into my neighborhood and other kids next to my modular home began to come out and play. The four Medina brothers, who were Mexican-American, lived to the right of me. They had been living there; I just never saw them come out.

Of those Medina bothers one was in my grade, going into second grade. I learned that the brothers would steal things from people's yards. They weren't afraid to break windows for the fun of it. One day I saw them jump a cranky white lady's fence and retrieve a soccer ball that was kicked over there. This happened on many occasions. To make matters worse, the Medina brothers grabbed thick branches and shovels and began hitting her shed, damaging it really badly, and then took off running.

Living to the left of me, across the street, was a Mexican boy named Vani who was younger than me. That young boy was just like me, very quiet and shy. Two doors in front of Vani lived the Rodriguez family consisting of two boys, one older and one younger than me, and their two sisters.

Those two brothers were like spotted hyenas. We referred to them as hyenas because they would laugh at everything even when I was trying to be serious. They sometimes would laugh just to annoy me and they continued to laugh at me as I tried to walk away.

The oldest Rodriguez boy, Ruben, was eight, and his younger brother, Eddie, was six. Ruben, Eddie, and Vani were mainly the kids I played with. We played soccer on the weekends from lunch time until dinner. We also played tag or sometimes I would go to Vani's or the Rodriguez' house to play video games. *Mi jefita* hated it when I went into the houses of other people, because she didn't want me to be a burden. She hated it more when I would tell her we would be outside,

13

fully knowing that I lied and would be inside playing games. Playing with the boys continued until the end of summer.

SECOND GRADE

Once summer had become yesterday, and today was the first day of second grade, I wasn't as worried because school would be a bit different. Handley School had multi-age classrooms. My second-grade classroom had second **and** third graders and that meant more students and one extra teacher. In my class I had Mrs. Frank. The third-grade teacher was Mrs. Free and, just like last year, this class didn't have any Hispanics.

I was expecting second grade to be the same as the year before because I didn't really have friends. So, I was anxious to just go home and play with my summer friends.

A few hours into my first day, the principal brought my hyena-friend Ruben Rodriguez to my class. Ruben only spoke Spanish so, instead of being placed in third grade, he got dropped into second grade.

This was a really great first day of school. In my class we had 40-50 students. We were seated at round tables with six to seven students. Our classroom was like two classrooms put together and in the middle of the room was a sliding door to transform it into two separate rooms. When we had story time, we would have to move some of the tables from the middle of the room to sit on the floor.

I didn't have a problem with anyone. Recess that year was different too. I thought there would be just a few Hispanic kids at recess, but that wasn't the case. Recess consisted of second **and** third grade kids, and there were a lot of Hispanics. There was even one I knew because my parents had known his family from when I was in Kindergarten.

Don't get excited here though. My life wasn't better or lived happily ever after.

At recess I hung out with the Mexican boys mainly because they played futbol every day. That was how I met some new kids. There were a few American boys who also played with us, but never really talked to any of us unless they wanted to play a game of soccer.

While the white kids wanted to know what I was, some of the Mexican kids asked me where I was born. So, I told them, "Illinois." Well that was not the answer they had expected me to say. They laughed at me and said, "O no nacistes en Mexico?" (Oh, you weren't born in Mexico?). "Tu eres un gringo!"

The laughter, facial expressions, and the pointing made me feel so uncomfortable that all I wanted to do was get home and hide. Seven-years-old, in second grade, and I was living a life of laughter, but instead of being some comedian child, I was the abnormal kid being laughed at. Recess had ended and I was the laughing stock among the Mexican kids. That day when I got home, I didn't cry. Instead, I sat in my room depressed and confused about myself. I came out and ask mi jefita why I was born in the United States. She explained to me they came to America to create a better life and opportunity. Also, to give me and my sister the benefit of being born in the United States. To me, being Mexican-American felt like being a freak. From that incident at recess, my friends, Ruben and Eddie, began cracking jokes about me.

"Mira, hay viene el gringo," (look, here comes the white boy), they would say to me as I came to play with them.

At age seven, I began to build hatred. I had some kids at Handley school who hated that I was Mexican and others hating that I was

American. I was trapped in the middle and unable to do anything about it.

A few months went by and I was still dealing with the racist slurs and comments from both sides of the ethnic line. One day my family and I went over to one of their friend's home to watch a soccer game on TV. They lived in a modular that wasn't far from us. The family had no children at that time, so I didn't have anyone to play with besides my sister, or go outside and wait for my friends.

I still hung out and played with the hyena boys, only because that was just about all I had. I didn't want them to see me get affected from what they said, so I just bottled up my feelings. Vani was a good kid. He never made fun of me. Ruben and Eddie were a different story. I never told my parents it was those two who said some of those mean things to me.

One day when I was playing with Ruben, Eddie, and Vani, the comments and bullying began again. After a few times of hearing their verbal stabs, the pressure I had bottled up inside exploded. I cussed and swung with all my might to connect with Eddie. Ruben jumped in fast to hit me a few times. Vani saw this and ran home so I was alone in a backyard with the hyenas where no one could see us. I didn't care what would happen at that point. In all actuality, I blacked out and didn't feel any pain or even realize what was going on. They stopped after a few seconds and I jumped up and ran to my parents' friends' house.

As I went inside my parents asked me what was wrong.

I said, "Nothing. We were playing and the soccer ball hit me and hurt me."

17

My parents told me to be careful because no one was watching us. The thing is, they had no idea what was going on when nobody was watching. I don't recall how the conversation between my parents, their friends, and me occurred, but they asked me what I wanted to be when I grew up.

Hot headed as I was after the beating, I verbally jumped at them and said, "*Yo quiero ser una policia para llevar los a la carcel y mandarlos a todos ustedes para Mexico.*" (I want to be a police officer so I can take you guys to jail and send you back to Mexico.).

Were my parents shocked with what I said? They thought I was joking and laughed. Being laughed at angered me more. Ever since the time I had been in Handley School, all I heard were people laughing at me. I told *mi jefita* and *jefe* that I was serious. I hated being Mexican, because kids didn't like me for being brown and Mexican. I also told them that Mexican kids made fun of me because I wasn't a true Mexican-born child. I angrily told my parents that I wasn't Mexican.

I yelled, "I want to be American!"

My parents were getting upset and explained to me why I was Mexican-American. They told me that the American kids disliked me for being brown and because I knew something more than they did. They told me the Mexican kids made fun of me for being American because I was born with citizenship and had the opportunity to do great things. I didn't care about the great things in the future though. I just wanted all this to stop now.

In the spring of 2000 while I was still seven-years-old, when I would go outside, I avoided Eddie and Ruben. To avoid them I wandered off my street a few blocks further where I learned my

18

neighborhood was a dangerous place to live. I began to etch things more deeply into my head about drugs and gangs. I also met other kids who were troublemakers...not the type of kids I wanted to hang out with when they were breaking car windows in broad daylight. A few times, when I walked further than my area, I got beat up. I learned at a young age I had to watch my own back…constantly.

There were a few times when *mi jefita* realized I was not where I said I was going to be because she went looking for me at Vani's or the Rodriguez' house. I discovered this the day I came home and she angrily asked me, *"Donde estabas?"* (Where have you been?).

"En la casa de Vani." (At Vani's house).

Mi jefita really got mad because she had already asked for me at Vani's and found I wasn't there. I told her I was running in his backyard with the other kids. She was furious and grounded me from going outside. The remainder of my second grade continued the same. Sometimes better, sometimes worse.

SCHOOL'S OUT FOR SUMMER!

How excited I was that second grade had ended and summer was here. No longer did I have to worry about the mean kids at recess. The names I had for them in my head were built with hatred for all the slurs they had said to me. It was summer, so nothing to worry about for the next two and a half months, except Ruben and Eddie.

That summer Ruben, Eddie, Vani and I played again as if nothing ever happened before. The only difference was that this summer I would wander more and explore. I felt trapped and stuck with the kids I was hanging with. I needed to break away from the pressures of being categorized as either a gringo, a Mexican or neither. It was amazing to see that I could go further than the confines of the dead-end street I was on. It was exciting but also scary because my mom told me not to go beyond certain boundaries. But somehow, in that neighborhood, it was hard to do because of *los borrachos* (the drunks). They were the ones that I saw cause destruction. There were nights, and I mean many nights, where you would hear them partying, yelling, and even firing guns. I thought the police would come to calm down the situations, but yet the police never ever arrived.

One Saturday morning that summer, I was outside playing with the boys and saw three of those *borrachos* walking into my dead-end street. I was confused. When I saw them scatter, I knew something was wrong so, I ran into my parent's car. I jumped in the back seat and hid from the guys. I knew two of them and my parents knew their wives. That didn't matter to the *borrachos* though. One of them walked right up to *mi tios* (my uncles') apartment, across from my house, and knocked on their door. I saw *mi tio* peep out of his window. He did not open his door. Fear ran through me. Then I saw the guy swing and break a small window that was next to the door on the top right. *El borracho* pulled a knife and tried stabbing *mi tio* through the window, and after he couldn't get in, he walked away and was going to my place. I was even more scared after what I had just seen. I did what many would call crazy or stupid. I jumped out of the car, ran in front of him, and rushed into my house slamming the door right behind me. *Mi jefita* was in the kitchen and I told her not to open the door because there was a bad guy with a knife just outside. *El borracho* knocked on the door with anger-fueled poundings. *Mi jefita* looked through the window and saw who it was and she cracked the door open since she knew him.

El borracho angrily asked, "*Donde esta su esposo?*" (where's your husband?)

"*Se esta bañado y no puede salir ahorita,*" (he's showering and can't come out now), answered *mi jefita*.

"*Luego regreso,*" (I'll be back,) and he left.

I never heard anything after that, but I was freaked out that I could have lost my father. After a while, when the adrenaline rush slowed down, I realized why my parents never heard the window break across the way at *mi tios*. My parents always played music on the weekends and it was so loud you couldn't hear anything from the inside. I never knew why he was so angry at *mi tio* and *mi jefe*. That *borracho* never came back to my house, which made me relieved.

THIRD GRADE

Summer had ended which meant back-to-school, but for third grade this time. The encounters from the Mexican-born kids continued. A few times during the year I would get beat up at recess. Somehow the recess ladies, parents who volunteered to be monitors, always put my bully **and me** on the outside wall as a punishment. At Handley School if you were at recess cursing, fighting, or doing something you weren't supposed to, especially after being told once, they would put you in time out. Time out meant standing up on the wall with your eyes towards the rough red bricks. I usually ended up on the wall because I was trying to defend myself as I was getting hit. One time, in the cold weather, I got caught, but not the kid who had started picking on me. Boy was I angry.

On another occasion, Chris, one of the Mexican-born kids, was antagonizing me. He was shoving, punching, and even spitting all over my face. One of the kids he was with told him to leave me alone, but Chris wanted to make me cry, fight back or do something. I don't really know why he did this. We were standing by the bike racks when Chris gave me a hard push and I flew backwards hitting my head on the bottom of the bike rack. I was fired up with so much anger. I couldn't take it anymore. The pressure inside me erupted which caused me to pick up the closest thing I could find...a good-sized tree branch. Jumping up and grabbing the stick like a baseball bat, I swung and hit him on his side. He groaned and was furious but, by that time, the recess lady saw me with the stick. I explained what happened and she told me, because of the other few times I got into trouble for fighting, she didn't believe me, even though I was defending myself. So, I was put on the wall right after we finished lunch. I was forced to spend the next few days' recesses on that wall.

Some people might say, "Well who cares. You got recess the other days and life wasn't over, right?"

You'd be correct, but the bully got away with his cruelty. And, it didn't stop there. I was on the wall and, whenever the recess lady wasn't paying attention, he would come by and slam my forehead against the freezing bricks. A couple of times he even came and kicked the back of my legs so hard I would drop to the ground with a charley horse. I tried grabbing the recess lady's attention but she ignored me, or would yell at me and tell me to keep quiet! From that day forward I would avoid him and hide at recess if I had to. What third grader could enjoy recess like that?

When I went home *mi jefita* saw my forehead and asked what happened. I told her I had tripped and fell. She would get irritated and tell me that I had to be more careful or I was going to get "head trauma." Never did I tell *mi jefita* what happened at school or the times I got bullied on my way home. One of the times was when I got jumped twice after encountering older guys from a different neighborhood. I felt their knuckles and tip of their shoes hit my arms, legs, and back after being shoved to the ground. I never liked to fight and, when I did, it took a lot of anger like with Chris, to get me going and fight back. Those times, as well, I never told *mi jefita*. What I did to avoid getting jumped every day instead was to change my routes home. I would run through the school yard, then down an alley, and curve around to my house. Man, how I hated doing that daily.

Close to the end of third grade, my parents began talking about moving. Even though I was bullied where we lived, I didn't want to move. Why you may ask? Well, you see, I knew this school and knew my way around and how to avoid situations. I didn't want to relearn everything again to avoid being bullied.

FOURTH and FIFTH GRADE

During summer break my family moved to a neighborhood where it was nice and calm, or so I thought at that time. I looked around and there were elderly people, no *borrachos*, just lots of quiet. It didn't seem to have any kids around though. I didn't know if that was a good or bad thing since, for some reason, I missed my old neighborhood because I knew where to go and what to avoid. I knew the people. I didn't know anyone here.

After a few days I realized I had two neighbors to the right of my house who had kids. I didn't really try talking to them and rarely saw them outside.

When summer was over, and I was getting ready to start the fourth grade at the Hailmann school, I was nervous. I looked around and didn't see any other Hispanics. I thought, "Oh no, this is all going to happen again." But within few minutes a Mexican girl showed up and I didn't feel out of place. I didn't try talking to her though. I stayed to myself. I didn't want to make new friends because I was frozen within my skin from all the bullying I had endured. That whole year flew by with no problems which was very different for me. I was just going to school, coming home, doing homework, and practicing soccer in my backyard.

Fifth grade, the start of the new school year, I was as worried about what would happen as I had been so many other times. The year before I had made a few new neighborhood friends, and they were not Hispanic. They didn't care that I was Mexican which was odd to me. They said as long as I wasn't racist toward them, they didn't mind me. I felt relieved because I had never heard that before. I was more at ease. No worries.

In fifth grade I'd come home, do my homework, and as soon as it was done, I would go outside and play with a boy who lived two houses down and we had become friends. His name was Alex. He was non-Hispanic and liked to play baseball which was something different for me, but I didn't care. I had befriended him and four of his buddies. That became our thing...going to school, coming home and looking forward to playing baseball in Alex's backyard. After a couple of weeks of this being a routine, I felt I was in a safe situation. But then I learned it didn't matter where you live because every area had its problems.

I remember one nice warm spring day with birds chirping and the smell of rich green grass near where we were playing baseball. Everything was wonderful and then...these three white boys walked by Alex's house. Calvin, a year older than me, was short and skinny just like me. His brother Harry, two or three years older, was tall and wiry. Their cousin (I never knew his name) was about the same age as Harry and he was about my height but more on the stocky side. When they reached the front of Alex's house, I saw Alex and the other guys scram, so I did as well. I hid behind a tree on my yard and peeked to see if the guys were playing around because I didn't know why they ran. My friends never came back, so I decided to go inside.

The next day I learned why my friends took off running. They told me that Calvin, Harry, and their cousin were in a gang and were always getting into or causing trouble. My friends actually said, "If you see them coming over here when we are playing, run. You do not want to get stuck here with them."

A few times after learning who the guys were, I stayed on high alert. Still, mind you, I never told my parents what happened and how we had to run and hide.

THE WORST DAY OF MY LIFE

This running away crap happened a few more times when Calvin and his crew showed up. The worst was on one warm spring day.

I had agreed to meet Alex and the guys at a specific time to play a little baseball competition in the backyard. We were deep into on our second game and not noticing anything other than trying to score runs. *Mi jefe* drove through the alley and called out of the car window, asking me if I wanted to stay or go with him and pick up *mi tia* (my aunt). I said I'd stay because we were still playing so he drove off.

We continued our baseball game...swinging bats, connecting with the ball, and running around bases. Then out of nowhere, Calvin and his crew showed up through the alley and were no more than 15 feet away from us. As soon as we saw them, we scattered. You could hear Calvin, Harry, and their cousin...demonically laughing as we ran. Since those guys came from the back, I didn't try going through my backyard and into my home. Instead, I ran around the front of Alex's house, past my sixth-grade neighbor who always complained when my soccer ball would go into her yard. And then I rushed into the front enclosed screen porch of my house. As soon as I got into my porch, I attempted to open the front door, but I couldn't open it. The front door was locked and I then began to hear laughter from the three guys. The guys were going over to the complaining neighbor's house, but right when I heard laughter I dropped to the floor of my porch. I was freaking out, because I'm crawling and stretching my arm to get the door knob and still trying to open the door. I just couldn't believe it was locked. That door knob would not turn.

I sat on my porch for a few minutes just listening because I had made a decision to leave the porch, cross in front of my neighbor's house, when there was no more activity, and get to Alex's house. I opened my front screen door and peeked out. Calvin and his gang weren't there. Nobody was in front of my neighbor's house, so I decided to make my move. As soon as I got to the front of her house, I heard the neighbor girl, and the three guys, laughing. The sound was coming from the back of her house.

The three boys and the neighbor girl were right around the corner of her house and I began to panic because I did not want to get beat up. Harry saw me and told me to hold on and not move. He then told me to come to him in front of my neighbor's house where they were chilling. Harry was checking me out and noticed I was trembling. Who wouldn't when you are by yourself at such a young age? I was in panic mode. I was so freaked out I didn't pay attention to who it was who said to me, "You aren't going nowhere today." I knew something was going really wrong.

The other two guys who were with Harry walked right up to me and gave me a little push back and forth making me tilt one direction and back the other. I would try stepping back and moving away and they would yank me closer. I finally froze. I didn't know what else to do. Do I fight back and defend myself? How much time do I need to run after I hit one of these guys? Or, do I stay here and take the beating? So many thoughts were running through my head that tears began to accumulate.

I told Harry, "Please, can I just leave?"

He uttered a jester's laugh and then said, "Who the fuck do you think I am to just let you go?"

With the words that came out of his mouth I feared for my life a little more. Then the unexpected happened which made me feel like my life was coming to an end. Harry pulled a gun out of his pants. His gang started cheering him on, jumping around like kids on a trampoline.

I didn't know what to do but beg for my life. "Please don't do this, please let me go!" At this time tears were falling out of my eyes as I prayed to be able to escape from him and his gun. I thought about running and wondered how far I'd be able to make it without getting shot. I stood there for what felt like an eternity and, in reality, was probably around ten minutes. Then Harry placed the gun directly against my forehead. I had my eyes closed and I prayed for an elderly person to come out to their yard and yell at us, but there was no one. I didn't hear a car or anything. I was alone, gone...probably dead. Then Harry said, "You are dead, motherfucker!" Then he shot the gun, BANG! The bullet hit the ground near my left foot.

Disoriented and with my eyes still closed tight, I slowly began to open them when I heard Harry say, "Get the fuck out of here before I blast your life away."

You see, at that exact moment, I didn't know who, or what, protected me, but Harry had changed his mind and shot about two to four inches away from my left foot into the dirt ground. I was so thankful and terrified I bolted to Alex's house. Banging on the door like a three-a.m. swat team trying to get Alex to open the door. He peeked and I yelled at him, "Let me the fuck in now!" He asked me if it's only me, by myself, and I said, "Yes now let me in."

30

When I got into his house I was still crying and yelling at him, "Didn't you hear the damn gun shot?" He said he had heard it, but wasn't going to go out there or make a call. I just stood there in shock and confusion like, "That was my life and you weren't going to call the police?"

Well it didn't matter much because I was trying to keep a look-out for my dad to come back home. Every time I peeked out for the car to be in the front it wasn't and I looked out the back and didn't see the vehicle either. I was anxious to just be in my home so I could sleep it all out. That was all I wanted.

About half an hour went by and Alex's dad came home and saw me still crying a little. He asked me, "What's wrong?" Instead of telling him the truth I replied, "Oh, I just found out some one in my family passed away," and left it at that. Alex was shocked with the response I had given his dad. I didn't care because he never planned on calling the police anyway.

We both had a fear about the old phrase...snitches get stitches. I stayed at Alex's house for quite some time. When it got dark I felt it was time for me to leave. Hopefully my dad would be home.

I told Alex to keep a look out for me as I went out the back door and to yell if he saw Harry and the others. I sure as hell didn't want to run into them again.

We moved Alex's sliding door and peeked. No sight of any of them but I could hear faint talking coming from the front of my neighbor's house. I knew it was time for me to head home so I bolted and ran through the alleyway, around my garage to my house.

"I'm home!" I said in my head with relief.

I walked right inside and my dad was making late dinner for us.

He asked, "*Donde estabas?*" (Where were you?)

"*Estaba en la casa de Alex porque las puertas estaban laqueadas.*" (I was at Alex's house because the doors were locked.)

Mi jefe giggled, "*No, yo deje la puerta de atras des laqueada para que tu podrias entrar.*" (No, I left the back door unlocked for you so you'd be able to get back in.)

I felt stupid but knew I had no chance anyway of getting to the back when my first reaction was to make it to the front. *Mi jefe* saw my red face and asked why it was all red. Just like Alex's dad I lied to my father.

I told him that I was running and exhausted myself even though, in his mind, he knew I wouldn't be that exhausted from only running from two houses down.

That night I went to my room and stayed there replaying that day over and over. I never wanted to experience that feeling of having a gun to my head again but I could never tell anyone about it, and I decided I wasn't going out for a while. The rest of the school year, and that summer before sixth grade, I stayed mostly inside and rarely went out even to my own backyard.

MIDDLE SCHOOL

August had arrived which meant my first day at Kesling Middle School was here. I was going to be riding the bus and I had to wait at the corner two blocks away. I wondered if Calvin was going to be around. I stayed on the lookout constantly and there was no sight of him or Harry. Finally, I got picked up by the bus and I was off to school.

In middle school it was a bit different. More districts were together which meant more kids, but I was hoping I would be back with the old Kingsporte neighborhood group. As I looked around I didn't see any of them. At the end of the day I found out they had switched from Handley School to another middle school.

I was out to make new friends, well a few, because I still had the friends from Hailmann school.

In sixth grade life felt easy for a while but just like in the past, I also seemed to fall under someone's bullying eye. I began getting teased and bullied but mainly from two students in gym class; only because that was the only class I had with these two guys. I tried so hard to avoid them but when you're in the guy's locker room, it's like an open field. Nobody cares what happens behind those closed doors. The gym teachers were nice but as soon as they would shut their office doors it was on. The two guys would come to the bench where I was even though their gym lockers were on the far corner of the other side.

"Hey brown boy," they would say.

Those little words I could ignore. They bothered me, but I was able to ignore them. But when they would start making Mexican slurs like,

"I bet he's good at jumping since he jumped over the fence to get to the United States.", then I would become upset.

.That irked me so badly. But, as usual, I would hold it all in. They would push and shove me. I dealt with it for a while and, even during lunch, when we were all there. Man, the only thing saving me during lunch was that their lunch table was two rows ahead of mine. In Kesling, you would come in and sit in your assigned seats. Then the lunch supervisors walked around and would call out the row of lunch tables who could then go to get their food. The lunch supervisors went down about six rows of tables. At lunch I sat with a couple of kids I knew but they never really talked to me as much as I tried talking to them. I would get heard for a few seconds and then nothing. When they talked about things they were going to do over the weekend, or what they did, and I couldn't relate with them. It put me in a different place so I'd be quiet. Occasionally I was able to converse about relative things, but for the most part, that whole year, I just sat there and dealt with getting pushed around, being verbally abused by the bullies, and being a loner.

INITIATION

The following year, a kid from Arizona who was in a gang down there, moved to LaPorte and started school at Kesling. This kid was Mexican-born but raised in Arizona at a young age. He knew English really well, but he wasn't your typical *"Cholo"* (Mexican gangster). He didn't wear creased up Dickies, button ups, or Cortez shoes. That was the stereotypical *Cholo* style. This kid just wore regular jeans and a t-shirt. You could consider him the class clown because he always tried making people laugh. I first met him in gym class.

He looked at me and said in English, "Ay brown skin homie, what's up?" In my head I thought great. Another guy to pick on me.

"My name is Armando what's yours?" he asked.

I was polite but cut it short by responding, "Victor."

He was all excited there was another Mexican in gym with him. That same day I saw something different...the reaction he had when people talked about our ethnicity.

Two guys came up to me and made a snide comment saying, "Oh, I see you made friends already. Figures it would be with another wetback."

It frustrated me but I saw Armando just looked shocked. He saw me react but by that time he just made a joke saying, "I don't know about Victor, but I am."

The guys weren't expecting someone responding to them like that and replied, "Maybe both of you guys should never have gotten wet and stayed there."

As they walked away, Armando was like, "Forget about them."

I tried acting like everything was fine and responded, "Oh I ain't worried about those fools."

For the next couple of weeks gym class wasn't too bad. Although maybe it was for the bullies because now they had two people who would stand up to them. Yes, I was saved, but not entirely. Gym was one thing lunch was another.

During lunch, Armando sat with a different group of guys...friends he had made in his first class on his first day. A few days later a new group of bullies started causing trouble. They were able to sneak around and go in the lunch line when I did. They basically waited for me to get into one of the lines without me knowing.

Our lunch room was set up with the cafeteria centered in the back and there was a short hallway that led to side doorways into the cafeteria, and in front of the cafeteria were all the lunch tables. So, on this day they followed me up in line. They weren't directly behind me, because I was talking to one of the people in line but always kept a lookout from the corner of my eye. When you are being bullied and harassed, you have a knack for being on guard.

At some point, as I was walking forward, both of the guys came up behind me and shoved my head into the wall's rough-edged brick. Then, one stuck his foot out while the other yanked me down to the floor. The pain I felt, the massive headache, had me on the floor for a second. When I looked around, I saw some of the other kids in line just staring at me, doing nothing to help, while I laid on the floor. Two of the bullies were laughing at me. I couldn't believe my eyes. Nobody said anything or extended an arm to help me up, or even ask if I was okay.

Emptiness, nobody caring, that's all I saw. I was beginning to develop a cold heart for people. I stood up, went to the back of the line and, grabbing my head, I proceeded to get my food but I was so angry I couldn't eat.

When I got home I just locked myself in my room. My parents didn't question anything much after awhile because it had turned into a daily routine. I would get home, lock myself up in my room (in the basement) and do my homework. I would come up to get dinner and swoop back downstairs. That day I had so much anger I didn't know how to let it out.

Even though the basement had stone walls I began bare hand punching them. One punch, two, and so on. I lost count. After awhile my hands became numb and I couldn't feel pain which frustrated me because I still had anger inside. I remember seeing the blood on my hands and just knew that I could cause myself pain in another way. I then grabbed a razor blade that was in the basement; yes, it probably wasn't new or sanitary, but I didn't care. I looked at the back of my wrist slightly touching my skin with the blade and strummed it like a violin. A thin slit was created on my wrist. It was a little less painful than a paper cut but, for some reason, it made me feel better. That day I created self-infliction and liked the fact that my pain was washed out...as if when the blood came out, so did whatever pain that happened to me that day.

Around that time I used to wear sweat wrist bands which made hiding my cuts easy. I cut my wrist a couple more times because of the number of mental breakdowns that haunted me as I relived the terrible things said and done to me. During one of those days Armando came up to me and randomly asked me if I knew he was running a local gang. I had heard about it, but I acted stupid, like I didn't know anything. He explained to me about the gang and said he saw something in me built ready for destruction. Whatever that meant. He was trying to recruit me and said he and the gang would have my back. They'd be my protection. That it wasn't about selling drugs but about unity and becoming a family. At that point, even though I was going through troubles, I said, "No disrespect, but I'm good right now bro."

He extended the offer and told me if I ever wanted to join to let him know. You see, I was always told, and just knew, not to join a gang. That joining a gang would cause more trouble no matter what. I thought about my family and I thought to myself, that I didn't want to join a gang because it would cause harm to my family.

About a week later from the recruitment attempt, I was late to lunch. The guys who I had problems with were in that lunch line. They were about five people ahead and, when I saw them, I tried turning around and going to the other line but one of the lunch ladies saw me and said, "No switching lines stay there."

When I got called out the bullies saw me and now I felt doomed because they had a grin on their faces from one side to the other.

"What's up wetback *beaner*?" they said. "Your stupid Mexican ass didn't get allowed to switch lines."

I was beginning to get heated. It was all building up and, in my mind, I wanted a razor blade to cut my wrist and wash away the pain. But no, that wasn't possible. Instead I switched it up. I erupted and called him out.

"What the fuck man, you are always fucking getting on me and pushing me around, what the hell is your problem?"

One of the guys dropped his grin and came up to me angrily saying, "What the fuck did you just say?"

At that point I had fear but I didn't even care anymore, "You heard me," I said.

He told me not to ever speak to him again unless I want to get beat up. So, what did I do? I shoved him so hard he went flying backwards. His buddy, pissed off, starts yelling and one of the lunch ladies sees this. She told him to continue walking and get his food, because there was a huge gap growing in the line. He yelled at me.

"Just wait until later fucker!"

As for me, I turned around since I had lost my appetite. When I was heading back I didn't go straight to my table. I went to Armando's table and said, "I need to talk to you right now."

He told me to sit next to him in the empty seat since one of his buddies wasn't there.

I flat out told him, "I'm in, under one condition."

"Shoot," he said.

"I need protection today!" I exclaimed. I then explained what happened.

He simply said, "Okay, we got your back. Tomorrow you come and sit over here and get initiated."

I didn't care about any other thoughts at that point. Those feelings I had about never joining a gang, that I would never do that, plus my concerns for my family, and the consequences, all went out the window.

At the end of the day, when I was walking out to the bus, I met up with Armando. We were talking and as soon as we walked into the side lobby, before going out to the buses, the two guys were waiting for me. We walked right past them. They were just staring and pointing at me. Armando raised his hands and said, "What, you got problems?"

They replied, "Not with you, with that fucker," pointing at me.

Armando told them, "Well now you've got problems with me and my crew if you have problems with him."

Armando went to his bus and I went to mine. I sat on that bus with no fear. Because of my new family, my problems immediately felt like they were being carried away. Nevertheless, I thought I still needed to watch my back.

The next day at lunch I walked right up to Armando's lunch table and was presented with all the information about the gang. The colors, saluting, hand signs, and I had to memorize all of them. If not, I would get a beating for discipline. As crazy as it seemed, I would join a gang to protect me from beatings, **but** I would receive them from the gang if I didn't obey their rules. It didn't bother me because I had a sense of family, someone who cared and watched over me outside of home, which to me at that point was more important. Armando told me for the initiation I would get three punches anywhere but the face from three of the members and that was it. I had no choice of where the punches landed.

"Alright I'm down," I said. We waited until we got in the lunch line far enough where nobody could see us. I remember them asking me if I was ready and one of the guys telling me to take my arm out of my sleeve. As soon as my right arm was exposed there were two rapid punches to that arm and then one to my side. The punch to my side

buckled me a bit and I just stood right up and said, "Come on bring it."
I didn't care that I was getting punched or beaten at this point because I
was gaining a family. The next guy was up and he pre-warned me of
where he was going to hit me, but he switched it up on me at the last
second. I got punches on my gut and thigh and more than just three
punches. I was confused at the amount of punches because it was
supposed to be three but again, I didn't care and just went with it. They
were all laughing because they knew they weren't going to just punch
me only three times if they didn't want to. The last guy took a few
rapid punches to the same thigh. Then punches to my gut and chest. At
this point I was aching but, the thing was, as soon as the last guy took
his final punch to my chest, he nodded to the person behind me.
Taking the punches from the third guy had me concentrating on him. I
didn't know who was where, but Armando was the one who threw the
final punches from behind. After the hits were over, everyone was
laughing and someone said, "I bet you're aching right about now."

I nodded. They then saluted me with the gang's handshake and that
was when I knew I was in this and now it was time to prove myself.

GANGS

Many teens who get initiated into gangs get an adrenaline rush running through them that lasts for a while. My adrenaline was off the charts for a few days because I now had a *protector family,* people who had extreme love to be there to stand up for me when I needed help.

The bullies stopped bothering me for a short time. Probably more for the fact they now saw I wasn't alone anymore. I also began drawing the gang's initials on my notebooks, book bag, my clothes and even my homework. I put the initials in the top corner of the paper, but my teachers never noticed, or if they did, they never said anything. When new people would start to pick on me, I had this new sense of power. I exuded, *you can't touch me or call me names.*

I belittled anyone who would try to put me down, even teachers. My seventh-grade literature teacher didn't like me speaking Spanish to a new student who could hardly speak English. I would translate for him and the teacher would tell me to *not speak that language.*

I told the teacher, "Fuck you man," and continued helping the student in Spanish. Normally I would have obeyed, but now I did as I pleased. I had power; at least it felt like it. There were times when the teacher would keep me after class and talk to me about why I was being so rude. I no longer cared about the way I spoke to others. I just didn't give a shit.

I told that teacher to her face one day, "Because your bitch-ass don't allow me to speak to my peers when they need help in our native tongue, you fucking suck at teaching. Because when we try correcting you, you want to keep denying that we are correct. So, fuck you."

That day I was trying to walk out of her class and she tried yanking me from my zip-up hoodie.

I just slipped right out of the hoodie and let her fall back on the desk telling her, "I will get that hoodie back motherfucker. You fucking watch me."

Other teachers heard me cussing and were shocked because they knew I was never that kind of an outspoken, disrespectful and profane person. Two teachers asked me if I was okay and if something was wrong.

I simply replied with, "I'm perfect" and gave them a grin from hell. Some people would say it was like looking into the eyes of an entirely different person without physically being able to tell.

I went to two more classes with a smirk on my face for what I had done. I had no remorse for my actions. In those two classes I didn't pay any attention because I was plotting on a way to get my hoodie back.

As soon as that third class ended, I blended in with the rest of the students and walked right into her class again like one of the next set of students she was going to teach. She must have gone to another classroom or something because she didn't know I was there. The students asked me what I was doing there since they thought I already had her class.

"Shh, you didn't see me in here," I said. I was searching quickly for my zip-up hoodie and found it under her desk. When some of the students saw me grab it, they told me she was going to find out and I would be in deep shit. I just told them to tell her I said, "I told you bitch, don't fuck with me."

As I walked out of her class, I saw her coming out of the computer lab which was two doors down from her classroom. She yelled at me, saying I wasn't allowed to get my hoodie back. I verbally insulted her and told her, "You don't fuck with me. You either take my shit, and I get it back, or you get a worse outcome."

She asked me if I was threatening her and I told her that I wasn't, I was just promising I would get my stuff back. Every time from that day on, she kept a close eye on me in class.

THE BULLIES ARE BACK

A few days after the altercation with my teacher, I was alone and was confronted by the kids who had been bullying me. The difference this time was that they had added a few new guys creating another ethnically-mixed gang. At the time I didn't know if it was mockery, or if they were seriously trying to build something. I found out when I overheard one of their new members talking to a girl in my class. He was bragging about their gang. I stopped him in mid conversation and was like, "Hey are you rolling with these guys?"

He replied, "No it's me and my buddy. We call ourselves, Blood Brothers."

I had a feeling he was lying to me, so I told him, "If you are creating a gang, you'd better drop it because *we* run this school and you will be responding to us."

He told me he wasn't in a gang and not to worry. He was cool with me and wouldn't go against me. That day I told our gang we needed to gather information because I heard there was a new gang coming about. The next day, sure enough, we found out my old bullies created a gang and that kid lied to my face. I had this urge to mark up as many things as I could so the rest of the school would notice and realize *we run this*. During my classes I drew on the desks and back of the seats. I would take razor blades and carve on bathroom stalls and desks. In gym class, when I was with some of the rival new gang members, Armando and I were always watching our backs.

That kid in me who was fearful of being bullied disappeared. He now had no fear whatsoever about getting hurt anymore. It was as if I enjoyed feeling that pain more and more. A few times we would flash gang signs back and forth, but Armando always wanted us to wait until we were more ready to do something. Armando wanted me to recruit more people because we were quickly getting outnumbered. I didn't mind recruiting. In fact, I felt honored to be given this important role in the gang.

As all of this went on, my family noticed I was acting differently. But, when they would ask, I continued to deny it all. My parents would sit me down to talk about how rude I was becoming. I would come up with excuses like, stressed from school or too tired and cranky as a way to quickly reason why I was like that. Sometimes I would simply say, "*Haci soy*," (that's just me).

My parents would try to show me they were there for me if I ever wanted to talk about anything, but by this point I already had a *family for protection* and also found ways to relieve my pains...self-infliction.

When people say my parents must have not been there to guide me or maybe didn't care for me as much, it makes me laugh a little. My parents were both there, married together in the same house, and they cared for my well-being more than you'd think. I just couldn't ever tell them the things that were really going on.

RECRUITING

Recruiting new members was the easiest thing because I knew who to look for. We weren't looking for the strongest, buffed-out kid...well, at least I wasn't. I was looking for the troubled kid, the one who was constantly getting bullied. The ones who felt like their world was ending. The ones who had family problems and anyone who felt like they were *nothing* in this world.

I was going to guarantee them the world, our family, our gang. That is how easy it was to pull members in. Our gang was growing and growing rapidly. We had guys from the high school, drop outs, and even elementary fifth graders.

Our name was getting known and these kids were starting to hear about us and know who we were. We loved that. It used to be that I had to walk around people on the streets, now they would have to walk around me. At first I thought, you know, people just being nice moving out of the way. But no, later I noticed it was because they knew what I represented...as I flashed my colors.

I remember one time my dad and I were walking in a store and he had said, "Excuse me," to these group of teens probably a year or two older than me, who were standing in the aisle. I looked at him and nobody moved. I walked up and, when they saw me, all except one, moved and that one guy got yanked back. He said to his buddy who wouldn't move, "Don't you know who he is? He is part of that one gang."

I had this smile on my face because I felt powerful over a simple thing and my dad didn't understand what happened. There were even kids at school who thought they were high and mighty. They wore expensive brand-named clothes and things. I bullied them by making fun of what they were doing. I talked down on their appearance making them feel like the expensive items they wore weren't going to make them any cooler or more attractive. When they tried reversing the insults to me, I would laugh and tell them I didn't care because I felt I had greater things.

I would find the kids who felt like nothing. I made them feel special and eventually recruited them into the gang. I remembered what it felt like to feel like that, so I knew how to talk to them. But what they didn't know is, I was still cutting to relieve some of the pain I felt. I just didn't do it as much.

USING MY POWER FOR GOOD

There was an incident in a seventh-grade class where I was able to use my power for good.

I was dating a girl who overheard a guy telling her friend that he was going to hit her. I overheard a bit of it too. I told him nicely to just calm down and forget about all that. I sat back down and heard him arguing again. The teacher had stepped out of the classroom so there was no one to protect the girl. I stood up and tried to get him to calm down. At this point this kid raised his hand at her. I ran up on him and shoved him, furiously telling him, "If you lay a hand on her I'm coming after you. I will kill you if you beat her."

He was in disbelief. He called me out, "Are you threatening me?"

I responded, "No I'm not, I'm making a promise homeboy."

When the teacher came back, he told the teacher he didn't feel good and needed to go see the nurse so she excused him. I knew this kid was faking it and so did the other kids. They warned me and said you know he's going to snitch on you.

I had no fear. I told my peers, "It's okay, he will get his if he does."

Fifteen minutes before the end of the day in that class, the teacher got a call from the principal's office, asking for her to send me down.

Normally, when you got called to the principal's office, the students would jeer at you and make noises meaning, *You're in trouble.* Not this time. Instead, as I walked past a few of them, they just said, "He ratted you out." I told them to find out if he had snitched on me and to tell him I'm on him.

When I walked into the principal's office he shut the door and asked me if I knew why I got called down. I acted like I knew nothing and said, "No." He told me I had threatened a student saying I was going to get some people to jump him. I smirked and told the principal that I told the kid I was going to hit him if he touched the girl because he raised his hand up to her. I explained that I don't like that type of disrespect and the principal let me walk out of his office by saying I had to be careful of the words I choose to say. I said, "Don't worry. I got it." I smiled right at him because he didn't know what I had exactly said to that kid.

From that day on I had that kid fearing for his life every time I saw him because I warned him to never call me out to anyone.

Putting a fear into people, like they did to me, made me feel good, like I was in control.

RUMBLE?

Problems started to crop up as the weeks went by. The guy who bragged about his gang was getting cocky. He confronted me in social studies class saying he was going to be hunting our gang, one-by-one. Mad-dogging each other back and forth, I let him know if something happened to me or the gang, I would put him down myself because I just didn't care anymore.

Life to me was nothing more than hours. At any point I knew someone I had pissed off could run up on me from behind, cut me with a knife, and then I would be dead. I understood these consequences and I didn't care anymore. I felt, or believed, I was nothing without the gang.

At the same time all of this was happening, Kenny, a classmate who I categorized as a prep/rich kid, was discussing something with his group. I didn't like him because of his social status and I never talked to him.

His group started playing around and shoving each other. When they were shoving each other, he bumped into me. I grabbed him from the back and shoved him off of me.

"Watch what the fuck you're doing," I blurted at him.

He got pissed off and got in my face saying, "What are you going to do?"

As I was about to hit him, a student nearby grabbed me and told me to cool it because the teacher saw us confronting each other.

The teacher came over and told us to, "Calm yourselves and sit down. Class is about to start."

I told the teacher, while giving a dead-eye stare to the prep group's kingpen, Kenny, "Tell this fool to watch his back and never question me."

A few minutes later Kenny was talking to the guy who had been shoving everyone. I heard Kenny throw my name into it. I had tucked my hand in my pocket. I was holding my pocket knife in one hand, and a pencil in the other, both exposed for him to see. I told him, "Never fucking put my name in your fucking mouth ever again."
"Ooo, I'm so scared," he said.

"You fucking better be." I let him know that he wouldn't be going back to his family if he created problems with me.

At that point the teacher noticed us arguing again and moved our desks. As I was walking away from my original desk, I blurted out to him that he was one more strike away from *finding out*. I had no more heart to care about how I was making my circle of friends small and, instead, filling it with enemies fast. My peers feared me because they could see I no longer cared what I had to do to people to shut them up. Luckily, to that point, I had somehow avoided any interaction with the police.

SCHOLARSHIP PROGRAM

During that year, I met Mrs. V., a youth advocate for Purdue North Central College (PNC). Her job was to help students from low income families get into college.

In order to keep a low profile in school, and have my parents proud of me, I always did my school work. Many gang members have that same mentality. This could be why Mrs. V. selected me as one of the few to be in a scholarship program. To many this would be a dream come true, but for me, it wasn't of much importance. Since PNC is near my town, I didn't think making it in would be a big deal. Plus, I didn't think I was going to live past the age of 16 because of the problems I was creating in and out of school.

Mrs. V. would meet with us a few times a week. She'd catch up on how we were doing. Then, since our scholarship required us to perform community service hours, we'd discuss ways we could help the school. I'm mentioning her now because she later helped me out in life.

A GUN AND POLICE AT SCHOOL

Everything changed on the day one of our members took me and another member to a corner in the school. He told us he had brought a gun to school. He had gone hunting with this dad and forgot the gun was still in his book bag.

We told him to shut his mouth and not tell anybody. We asked him, "Who knew," and he said, "No one else, just us two."

I told him, "Keep it that way because you're going to bring us trouble."

A little later we met up with Armando and told him to keep that kid *on silence,* because he seemed too excited to have a gun on him.

Later that morning we found out that little homie got in trouble and I mean serious trouble. He ended up telling other kids about the gun and the school administration got wind of it. They called in the police who found the weapon in his locker. That's when they put him in the police car and took him to the station.

The homie told the police he took the gun to school because he feared for his life. He said there was a well-known local town gang who was threatening him and that's why he took the gun to school.

The kid, being one of our members, brought us trouble. Our school knew who we were and what we were. They also knew we were growing in numbers including older guys in high school, all still run by Armando. I was pulled out of class a couple days after that incident and had to meet with the principal and a police officer. I sat in a chair facing another chair only about three feet apart. I had my notebook with me that had gang taggings on it and my pants were marked up with gang symbols. Neither the officer nor the principal saw them though.

The officer didn't beat around the bush. He laid it down and told me he knew there was a gang in the middle school that was growing in numbers as well as recruiting in the high school. Of course, I thought in my head, *yeah, we're the ones recruiting them.*

He told me he had heard we were causing property damage outside and inside of school. He mentioned he'd also heard, from around the streets, that I was the shot caller. Hearing that caught me off guard. Me??? The shot caller??? I wondered why he thought that.

The officer asked me about all the talk about our gang. Armando had told me, if any authority questioned us, to deny it and tell them we are a clique of friends. So, what did I do? You bet I told that officer we were a clique of friends and we have never done any property damage to the school and if anyone had done that, they would be kicked out of our group. I was grateful he didn't ask about internal school damage to desks, chairs, lockers, tables and benches, of course, because, that was us.

The officer explained to me that, by the time we hit high school, if this gang was still going on, he was going to be on us. He told me that he had me on a watch list. If I got into trouble in high school by the age of 18 I would have a criminal gang affiliation record.

At that moment it didn't faze me. I didn't care. So, what? I didn't even know if I'd live to see my 18th birthday. The last thing the officer told me was that he wondered why I was even with this gang or, as I had said, *clique of friends*, since I didn't have a record, didn't get into trouble, and my grades were decent. But I knew it was because I just never got caught. I told him I was around these guys because they were my friends since I was young. I lied through my teeth right in front of the officer. The principal praised me to the officer and said I was a good student and was in a scholarship program. The officer told me to straighten up and get away from those friends, even if it meant being a loner. He obviously didn't know I was a loner for so many years. This gang, which was always referred to as family, loved me, protected me, and gave me a sense of belonging.

The next day we all met up at school and talked about what we had said to the police. That's where I found out everyone else got called in groups. I was the only one who got singled out. Luckily my story fit in with the rest of the gang, and we still continued to recruit.

This whole incident continued to cause trouble as our rival gang found out we were on thin ice with the police. They started spreading false information. They picked us out one by one. Some of our guys were getting their homes searched for guns and others for drugs. Luckily none had anything at home, so no one got into trouble. My name hadn't got picked for searching.

The hardest part for me was how to deal with *mi jefita*. One day she came home from work and asked, "Estas despierto," (are you awake?)

I said, "Si, Si estoy," (Yes, yes I am.)

Mi jefita told me a family friend of a gang buddy of mine told her to be careful of who I was around because their home was searched for drugs and guns. *Mi jefita* asked me if I had any. I said no. She had a long conversation with me and, even though she talked for a while, I didn't really listen. What I do remember is seeing her cry. She told me she didn't want me to be hurt or get in trouble.

I know she wanted me to have a future, but she didn't know everything I'd been through. She had no idea what I was involved with and that I might not even make it to 16 years of age. I went to sleep that night with a blank mind...nothing on my conscious.

LEAVING THE GANG

Near the end of the seventh-grade semester, three rival gang members followed me down the hall after my last class of the day. They started pushing me and calling me names, really getting into my head. I was ready to do a horrifying thing that could have led me into a cell. But...I held back. They tripped me onto the ground, hit me with a few punches and then walked off. What shook me up more than the punches that day was a fact I had learned about what it was like to be a member of a so-called family. When those guys tripped me onto the floor and hit with that first punch, one of my friends and fellow gang member walked past, made eye contact with me, and just kept on walking. I wasn't one to yell out for help, so I just took the hits and couldn't understand why he didn't help me.

When I got home, I replayed everything in my head. I was down for anything. If that was me walking past my fellow gang member I would have jumped right in. But that day, thinking about what happened to me while just a stone's throw away, someone from *my family* did nothing. I began to distance myself.

Some of the members started to freak out because police knew who they were. Our group began to lose power. They started to tell Armando they were out and it wasn't just one or two, no, we were losing numbers fast. I would try to salute some people and they said they were done. I, who followed the rules, was ready to discipline them until I found out Armando let them walk. That's when I knew it was falling apart. It was a couple of weeks later that our numbers were down to about maybe eight people from over 20 members. I walked up to Armando one morning at school and told him, "Look man, everyone has basically left and it seems more people are probably going to drop out. I'm telling you now that I'm done. I wanted the family I was told about in the beginning and, if I have to get out with punishment, let it be so, I don't care."

He looked at me and was shocked that I even made it this far with him. He let me walk and I told him, "If you ever need help, I'm still down, but I ain't saluting, repping, or none of that to symbolize the gang."

The girl I was with at that time was happy I was finally walking away from it. And, even though it wasn't like a huge gang, I had still created problems for myself. That meant I was back to being on my own, watching my back.

ONE LAST ATTACK?

I decided to focus on doing my school work and just getting by every day. I was doing pretty good until close to the end of the year. Two of the rival members, one which was my bully since sixth grade, Derek, got on my bus. I didn't know they lived close to me.

They started taunting me, saying they could make me do whatever they wanted because I had nobody. The thing was I wasn't afraid of them anymore or anyone like them.

I heard them tell a girl on the bus to watch because they were going to make me do whatever they said. Then they told me to open my bus window which extended the length of my seat and theirs, right behind me.

I said, "No, if you want to open it, you go for it." I was fine with the window the way it was so I didn't want to open it.

They got all pissed off and furiously told me, "Motherfucker, open the damn window!"

I just sat there and ignored them. I put my earbuds in and drowned my head with music. When we got to my bus stop, I got out and one of the guys on the bus yelled out for me to watch my back because Derek said he was going to do something to me. I looked back and saw the gang members get off the bus. I nodded at the guy who warned me and mouthed, "I know."

You see, when I put my earbuds in my ears, I didn't have it that loud so I could hear what they were saying because I knew they were riled up. They said they wanted to jump me when I got home so I was prepared. As I was walked to my house, which was two houses down from the bus stop, I kept my ears open for the speed of their steps. I knew if I would go through my front porch they would get me, so I decided to go through the back. As I walked through my grass one of them kept yelling out, "You pussy," telling me I was going to get it. Derek ran up on me and tried yanking me down but I let loose of my backpack. He began throwing punches and all I did was dodge them because in the back of my head I knew, if I get into trouble, the police could get involved and my ass is getting busted. So, I just protected myself and avoided as many punches as I could. Luckily none hit me, but that pissed him off. The guy then took my shirt and flipped it over my head but he still couldn't hit me for the duration of two seconds. He finally got my head in a headlock and I kept moving around. We neared a bush that was between me and my neighbor's yard. At this point I was feeling weak and short of breath from the headlock. Adrenaline kicked in and I grabbed his legs, lifted him up a bit and slammed him to the ground. He stayed down and I finally told him, and his partner, to get the fuck off my yard. I was so mad at myself that I didn't hurt him more because I was on the cops watch list.

When my parents came home I told them about what had happened. *Mi jefita*, freaking out, wanted me to go to the police station and make a report. I begged her not to. I told her *"Es mi problema y yo me encargo de esto"* (this was my problem and I would take care of it.) She said no and insisted I go and made my dad take me. I had no choice. We went to the police station and made a report. They said Derek wouldn't be allowed to come to my house and, if he did, they would arrest him.

Due to this entire situation I was frustrated at the gang members and

61

embarrassed by my parents for making me go to the police station to make that report. I was furious, disappointed in myself, and felt hatred towards everyone. With all of these emotions trapped inside, I got my razor blade and cut my wrist, arms, and legs to get the pain out.

The next day in school Derek and his partner told everyone he whooped my ass at my house. When people asked me if it was true I told them, "No that's not true, he couldn't even hit me, and not even with my shirt over my head."

They asked about a scratch on my eyebrow, I told them it was from a damn bush; he couldn't touch me at all.

My former gang members heard what happened and asked if I wanted to retaliate. I said no because karma will handle him.

That day we had a fire drill and, as we were going back into the school Derek was holding the door. As I was walked by he told someone to look at how he left me. I got mad.

"Motherfucker...you couldn't even touch me."

He said, "You want me to show you again?"

I told him to bring it, I wasn't afraid. Teachers heard us and made me continue walking and that was that for a while.

SUMMER BREAK

Summer had arrived and I was thankful because that school year had felt like an eternity. This summer I had planned on doing a lot of soccer practicing since that was the sport I loved playing ever since I was able to walk. Unfortunately, that's not how my summer played out.

It wasn't much after school ended that summer school began. I wasn't in summer school but Derek and his partner were, as well as one of the guys from my former gang. Those three were in the same class and must have been discussing something where my name popped up.

On a warm morning, I was at home playing video games and blaring music in the basement when my boy called me up worried. I asked what's up and he told me Derek and his partner were on the bus on their way to my house. They were mad and headed to my house to hurt me. I was laughing, not because what he was saying was a lie, but because I really wasn't worried...I was in my house. *Mi jefita* was upstairs and I was in the basement getting weapons ready...a handmade shank, a bat and some knives. I wasn't going to let someone come at me like this in my house, I thought. After getting the things ready I sat back, continued to play video games, and forgot about them coming over. I had the music blaring so I didn't hear them knock at the door. *Mi jefita* came downstairs and asked me if I was having friends over. I said, "No."

She started getting mad and asked me why there were two boys looking for me...one with a knife and the other looked like he had a gun.

I began smirking, "*O ellos. Yo no los envite pero sabia de ellos.*" (Oh those guys. No, I didn't invite them but I knew about them.)

Mi jefita, worried as hell, asked me what I meant when I said, *I knew about them.*

I told her my buddy said they were coming but I didn't know they would come with weapons like that. She made me stay in the house most of that summer unless I was travelling to play soccer on my team. I did, occasionally, go to the girl's house that I was dating, but that was it. *Mi jefita* just didn't want me to get attacked out in the streets. She didn't know I always stayed packing with a shank and a knife.

During the summer we had things around our house destroyed or someone would come by and would turn on the water hose and leave it by the house. Stupid childish things. Was it Derek? Possibly, but I had no proof.

EIGHTH-GRADE

When eighth-grade started I stayed more on my own. I didn't get close to anybody because I didn't know who to trust. Also, many didn't want to be around someone like me who was getting into trouble with gangs and police.

That whole year was a little bit calmer even though out in the streets, I would sometimes get chased by people I had previously pissed off or intimidated.

I remember one day, in broad daylight, I was with my ten-year-old cousin and my friend, who was also younger than me. We were walking around my area and some people recognized me. No colors, no gang signs, or anything that would show it was me, but they recognized me and jumped in a small truck, like an old Ford Ranger, and followed us.

I told the boys to stay quiet and run with me and not to fall behind. We took off running. They were freaking out and made me worried because, if they got hurt, that was on me. They wanted to run home and I said no because those guys didn't know where I lived so I was going to avoid going to my house. We ran through alleyways, one-way streets, and people's yards and finally lost them. We ran home and didn't do anything besides play video games in my basement bedroom. The only thing running through my head was, when will this ever be over? I almost got two young boys hurt because of me, and they weren't even part of the gang.

Towards the end of my eighth-grade year, the girl who I was dating for about a year and a half and I were done. It was a bad break up over a misunderstanding between her mom and me. So, when I was trying my best to get back to a "normal life" it wasn't happening. The break-up hurt me so bad the suicidal thoughts began rumbling through my head again. My cutting started again, and it became an everyday thing. I felt my life was ruined because she was my reason for living. I felt like there was nothing worth living for anymore because I had problems with people, and there was nothing else to live for.

Enter Mrs. V., the college prep coordinator, who called us all in, including my ex-girlfriend, for one last meeting before graduation. She talked about how high school was next and that we needed to make sure we continued making good grades in order to keep up our scholarships. She told us she would be there to help us along the way.

I was so depressed by the time summer break started, but knew I had to work hard and get through it.

A few weeks into summer break a positive turn around happened. Mrs. V called me and told me I needed to fill out the papers she had given us on our last visit of eighth grade. She explained this new scholarship would give me the opportunity to go to any accredited college in Indiana. Schools like Butler, Purdue, Indiana University and many others were now available to me. All I had to do was fill out this packet of papers. Thinking of the minimal chances of me making it to age 18, I procrastinated on filling them out. When I realized they were due within the next two days I immediately started filling them out. Why you may ask? This opportunity was hard to pass up now that I wanted to straighten out my life. The next day I called her and told her I was on my way. I jumped on my bike, and pedaled two and a half miles to get to the school. I was going fast because she was only going to be there for a few more minutes. I got there and she was happy I was going forward with this. So was I. Finally, I was making a good decision! When I pedaled back home I just took it easy and had a smile on my face. I knew I had something to work and live for now.

HIGH SCHOOL

Ninth grade, LaPorte High School, was a bit difficult even though I knew a few people and the old neighborhood friends from elementary were now at the school, we grew apart. I stayed a loner because the kids from the middle school didn't want to talk to me. They still remembered my time as a gang member.

What also began to hurt me was that my ex wanted to get back together. We tried for a few days and it wasn't the same. At first I felt elated she wanted me again, but then, when she found someone else, it caused me even more pain than before. I started having suicidal thoughts while in school. I'd go home and start cutting. Even though she was with someone else, she still wanted to talk to me which at that time, I thought was okay because I felt I still had a chance. But later I found out she was playing me which hurt me even more because I felt like I was being lied to. I really wasn't getting that chance. I found out the guy she was with, a 16-year-old sophomore, obviously didn't like me because I talked to her and he claimed to be a gangbanger.

So, just when I thought I was done with things, I wasn't because problems followed. This guy began to pick on me by pushing me, slapping the back of my head. If he found me outside of school he'd chased me with his adult brother-in-law.

One time, when I wasn't on my guard, they got me from behind and beat me up, telling me to stay away from my ex.

After that point, I dropped her completely. I wanted nothing to do with that anymore because it was ruining my life.

The rest of the year I was getting bullied by my ex's boyfriend even after she had broken up with him. He thought I made her break up with him which wasn't true. Life can sure take sharp turns into dead ends.

HOPE

One thing that brought some beautiful hope into my life was a nonprofit organization called Hey U.G.L.Y. which stands for Unique Gifted Lovable You. They helped me see so much within myself and in others. The organization helps kids around the world through their HeyUGLY.org website, school assemblies, Choose to Change Radio talk show and campaigns that deal with issues like racism, the power of forgiveness, negative results of gossip and much more. They also help to provide answers for people struggling with suicidal thoughts, bullying, and just any concern that brings down your self-esteem.

In 2008, towards the end of my ninth grade, Mrs. V brought Betty Hoeffner, Hey U.G.L.Y.'s cofounder, in to work with our group on the nonprofits' Hue-Man Being® ending racism art project as part of the community service hours.

Betty had our group of about 10 students stand in a circle with our forearms touching each other so we could notice how none of us had the exact same skin HUE. After discussing other things that were unique and different about each of us, we were asked to talk about common ground. It felt freeing to talk openly about how we may be physically different on the outside but we all have similarities inside...we all have a heart, we all bleed, we all have feelings. We talked about how kids can be bullied and how it affects the way they live life. Hearing the fact that I wasn't the only one going through troubles throughout my life made me realize I had something to live for. I didn't completely change that day, but I sure had a different mentality to life.

After the project was finished, Betty asked if anyone would like to be a guest DJ on Hey U.G.L.Y.'s Choose To Change Radio show, which has teen guest DJs suggesting songs with lyrics that inspire positive self-esteem, equality, a healthy planet, peace, diversity or never giving up. After they play each song, the DJ's discuss the message of the lyrics and how these songs can help youth all over the world *choose to change* things about themselves that may be holding them back from a life free of not feeling "good enough" and the self-bullying that results from feeling that way. She specifically asked me and I was afraid because that wasn't something I did. I decided to take a risk and said yes.

I was already doing music for awhile, producing beats, writing lyrics, recording, and just all of it, but I was doing it with home studio entry level equipment. Going into a radio studio and jumping over my nerves to have the courage to actually talk on the radio, was a challenge I wanted to take. I was scared to death when I walked into the studio and put on those big head phones. But, after a few minutes on air, it was like a bunch a friends sitting around talking about the lyrics of the song that just played. Betty said I was a natural!

At the time, the genre of music I wrote was rap and my lyrics were about money and being rich and famous, just like everyone on the radio was doing. After I met Hey U.G.L.Y., I definitely knew I had found my purpose to music. I changed my themes to lyrics that would help others. I had a street nickname that I went by for music. It wasn't until later that I changed my artist name. I'll tell you all about in a bit.

After that amazing experience with Hey U.G.L.Y., I got the awesome news that I qualified for the 21st Century Scholars program.

71

Everything felt like it was falling into place. The next year, 10th grade, was a lot easier. For me my past was in the past and I tried leaving it there. There were still times when trouble found me, but it wasn't that bad.

WORLDWIDE TV & QUEEN LATIFAH

In January of 2009 I was on Nick News with Linda Ellerbee; yes, NICK NEWS which airs worldwide on the Nickelodeon television channel. The producers wanted to interview some of us who were part of the Hue-Man Being Project and talk about diversity and being bullied. I was one of the few who were selected. At those moments, I didn't realize that things were signaling me of what one of my life purposes was to be.

Another amazing thing occurred, around May of 2009. My PNC College Bound scholarship group had participated in a community service competition and we were one of the winners. Different groups around the nation did things to help their communities and the reward was going to New York City to receive an award for the team. I got to experience a trip to New York City and it wasn't just going there as a vacation, it was an opportunity, at least for me, to see other people doing well. It was also a chance to see what kind of things they had done in their community so we could do the same for ours. On that trip I was able to meet some amazingly famous people, one of whom was **Queen Latifah**. She told us about the difficulties she dealt with growing up. This experience opened my eyes more and more as I began to see a brighter future for myself.

EDUCATING MY HATERS

In 2010, my junior year in high school, I was in an automotive class at a vocational school which was in another town about 20 minutes away. It wasn't just an automotive class. The school had different programs like nursing, computer engineering, small engine class, and welding. We had different students from my school riding this bus. I began getting called names from a few of the farm kids' clique, but I was able to talk and joke with some of the others.

There were these two kids who would make fun of me for being Mexican. Remember when I was younger in elementary school, I hated the fact that I was Hispanic but, as I got older, I learned that my culture meant a lot to me. I was proud of being Mexican because my family showed me dedication, never giving up, hard work, and more. This time, if I didn't like the way they were talking about me or my culture, I would defend it. Instead of just insulting them, I would try to educate them.

Many times they would say, "Oh you came here and don't pay taxes."

I'd tell them, "Well, for one I was born in Illinois and, for two, most of the immigrants who come here, if they get a fake social security card, they pay taxes and the government keeps that extra money."

They would say, "Yeah, but what if they have many dependents and we didn't tax them enough?"

"Well, that could be true, but many Mexicans would be afraid to do that because they didn't want to get the government on them," I explained. I wish I would have known then, what I know now which is that Mexicans who don't have real social security numbers lost all of the money they earned that was withheld by the government.

I also told these guys, "If they worked under the table and didn't pay taxes it wasn't just them not paying, it was also their employer. What about all the Americans who **are** citizens who also worked under the table?"

You see, they didn't like how I shot back with facts. This bullying went on for the whole year but I was learning to ignore it. Some days were worse than others though.

At one point, towards the end of the year, we were having problems with this kid from another class because he was disrespecting a girl. The farm kids knew I was with gangs before and told me about him. They thought that kid was awful and wanted me to shut him up. I tried to shut him up, not because of my former affiliation but for the fact he was disrespecting a human being.

From that day the farm kids didn't pick on me as much. However, they picked on other kids in my class though I tried stopping them. I told them to leave this one kid alone. I knew how bad it felt to be bullied, and the subsequent internal thoughts he would suffer.

COMMUNITY SERVICE

Community service hours were still always at play and they were worth it because it distracted me from causing self-harm. Yes, I still cut, but now it was only about once every two months or so.

Those community hours got me another chance to go to New York City again. This time I would be going with three other students from my group. We again learned what other kids were doing as we received our award. These awards, for me, weren't the actual little trophies we got, instead it was the opportunities I was given after all the craziness I had experienced and survived.

My senior year of high school was a lot calmer than my previous years. In the beginning, the kid from the vocational school that the farm kids wanted me to confront, was causing more and more problems in my automotive class. I was stepping back into the dark again because I wanted to retaliate and defend my classmates. I didn't like the fact that he was hassling my classmates and me for no reason. He had been the one disrespecting a girl and we didn't like that. He eventually transferred to my high school. I think he felt so uncomfortable when he saw me because he was in my territory now.

I didn't do anything stupid but occasionally, as he walked by me in the hall, he would try to shoulder check me. The next few times he tried he got the worst of it.

Eventually I found out he was part of a gang as was his family. That didn't put much fear into me though. It was more the fact of me wanting to survive to be at least 18 years old. That kid finally calmed down which was a good thing. We had no trouble from him anymore.

FALLING IN LOVE

I was working part-time at an urban clothing store called Ecko Unlimited. On one momentous day in August of 2010, this beautiful girl walked through the door and I remember thinking she had a spotlight on her. A natural thing for me to do at my job was to greet the customers.

So, I said, "Welcome to Ecko Unlimited. T-shirts are 2 for $30 today."

She smiled and looked away. I couldn't keep my eyes off of this beautiful girl. That day I got her phone number and immediately began talking to her. I had fallen in love. We would stay up and talk and talk for hours, even on school nights. She eventually became a piece of me and I wanted to be more than just friends. In October, we started dating and from there I had my reason to live. I wanted to give each and every day a chance because I saw someone I wanted to be with. Yes, I was still afraid because in my past relationships, I had been cheated on and it hurt, but I wanted to give it all I had with this girl.

I had told her I had, in previous times, caused self-infliction and she told me I was never allowed to do that again. Since my time was occupied on my girl, I didn't get into trouble. However, that didn't stop trouble from finding me.

POSSIBLE RACE WAR

In the beginning of spring 2011, a race war broke out between the blacks and Mexicans in my high school. The reason this occurred was because a few Mexicans had got into an argument with a few black students and things escalated. Eventually each was telling their people to get ready for a throw down. I remember telling my girl about it and she was not happy because she went to school in another town. I know if she would have been in my school, she would have stopped me from joining in on the fighting and that would have been the best thing.

The throw down was planned for the next day and it was getting bigger as people were getting recruited from outside of school including adults and families. The principal of our school even had the police on standby.

That day the assistant principal pulled me out of my class and asked me what this was all about. I told him it was a disagreement between a few guys that had escalated.

The assistant principal said, "I know you. You need to stop this immediately. Get these guys to stop because they will get in trouble with the authorities or, worse, someone could get hurt because I hear guns are involved."

I told the assistant I would honestly try my best to stop it but it was already so late in the day that it would be hard to do. I asked him to not hold it against me if I failed.

The end of the day came and police officers were posted outside, in front of the school. I was walking with the main Mexican guy, trying to get him to stop. I convinced him, as far as him saying that he would only do something if they start something.

Two black guys got on the bus, sat in the front and flashed gang signs. My guy immediately put his backpack down and stuck his hand inside of it. I glanced, saw a handgun and immediately jumped on his hand. I told him to not pull it out because there were many innocent bystanders on the bus. He was fighting with me to get his gun out and I kept trying and trying until he stopped.

I said, "Come on, let's drop this beef and go."

As we walked away one of those guys on the bus yelled something at us. The guy I was with flashed a gang sign at them. An officer saw that and started chasing him. I walked calmly away knowing he had fucked up. That kid got super lucky that they never found the gun. He only got in trouble for throwing gang signs.

Luckily for me nothing more happened. I was really glad not one person got hurt that day.

AUTOMOTIVE SCHOOL

That summer I was getting ready to go to a technical school. Yes, I know, all that hard work of community service for scholarships and I decided to go to a technical school????

I knew at that time I couldn't handle the stress of four more years of school and I wanted to be in and out, so I decided to go to an automotive school in Pennsylvania.

My girl, whose name is Nikki by the way, and I kept discussing about her going with me to Pennsylvania. We were trying to convince our parents that this would be a good thing. You see, she is younger than me by two years and two months and she was still in high school. I told them I would make sure she was in school out there.

We finally convinced both of our parents to let us be together in Pennsylvania. We were going to have her mom come out later to make sure Nikki would be okay living there and going to school.

Around the end of July in 2011 we both jumped into my red Dodge Neon and drove eight hours to a town we had never seen to look for an apartment and start this next chapter in our lives. It was heartbreaking for both of us to leave our parents, but I felt even worse because she was younger and leaving her mom, the only parent she had in her life besides me. I remember her crying because she missed home and I kept telling her, "I will turn around and take you back home." I felt so bad for her!

She stuck with me though, and said, "It's okay. I want this life with you." She brought joy to me! I promised my parents Nikki and I would go to school. I told them I would find a job, and take good care of us, so we could begin our lives together.

In the first two weeks we were there, I began applying for jobs. Something seemed different though. I learned some people really care about skin tones. I don't mind what color of skin you are; I will treat you fairly and I expect to be treated the same. Well, when Nikki (white American) and I went places, people stared at us. Everyone in this town was white, except me and one black person.

When I put in applications they would stare at me like I was an alien. It was weird getting that look because my automotive school, which was 30 miles away, had a multi-ethnic student body. So why did they look at me weird? Some treated me bad. They treated Nikki bad too, because she was with me. We would go to Wal-Mart and ask a clerk for help, looking at them directly in the eye. The clerks would just walk away. They would ignore us. In one of the places I applied, they told me they were short of help, yet after they saw me, said I wasn't qualified even though I had much experience in customer service and food service.

I had a great work ethic, so I didn't understand. I was walking away from the manager who told me I wasn't qualified when one of the workers pulled me aside and said, "She's lying to you. You are brown and she didn't want to have your race here."

Wow, I was in disbelief. I was 18 years old and adults were treating me like this because of my ethnicity. It was unbelievable the treatment you would get just because you were born that way. I didn't rant about it, but I did go home and tell Nikki. She was not happy. She said we should complain. I said not to, because karma would get them one day. It made me feel like giving up, because I had to ask my parents to assist me in paying my bills for gas, food, and essentials we needed.

AND BABY MAKES THREE

Around September, we had some news that changed our life even more. Nikki and I found out we were going to be bringing a little piece of each other into this world. I was scared because I didn't know what I was going to be doing. I didn't have a ready home for us, steady job, or things we needed to take care of a family.

When it was time to tell my family I was petrified because in my culture the man has to grow up and be able to provide for the family and I couldn't. Also, my family wanted me to be established with my career and have that steady job.

When we told them, they were a little concerned because we were young and they thought I was going to quit school. I told them I wasn't going to and that Nikki wasn't going to let me. They were disappointed because now Nikki wasn't going to finish school and they cared about her education as well.

Mi jefita was very caring because she wanted the best for me and Nikki. I remember crying to my mom as I was trying to tell her. Thank God she wasn't as disappointed as I had pictured she would be. *Mi jefe* told me, "*Ya es tiempo que los mantengas y busques duro por un trabajo.*" (Well, its time you begin taking care of them and work super hard to find a job.)

I told my dad I was trying but because I was Mexican, I was getting pushed away. One might say, "I doubt it was because of your race." Okay, maybe a couple of those applications you may be right. But, when you put in about 15-20 applications at fast food restaurants, a few clothing stores, furniture stores and anyone else hiring, and they all had signs saying help wanted, it was pretty clear my skin color separated me from others.

The treatment from the town was different too. Some people in public would give me dirty looks. Others told me to go back where I came from. Now they started doing that to Nikki, especially since she was *my* Nikki. It was weird for them to see two different colored people being together. We'd just kept walking, holding our heads up and went on with our business. It's crazy though to think adults who were probably 35 and older, treated an 18 and 16-year-old like this. It made us more mentally strong.

HIDING OUT AND LONELY

In October of 2011, Nikki and I went through a super hard time because the Pennsylvania Department of Children and Family Services (PDCF) found out her mom was still not living with us. Since Nikki was underage, she was not allowed to be there without parental supervision.

PDCF sent a notice to our house saying, if her mom didn't take her back to Indiana, they would put her in foster care. I was furious, depressed, and scared. I didn't know what to do. She was pregnant and I wanted to help her and take care of her. I remember we had to put up black garbage bags over the windows so no one could peek in while I went to school. We had only one car so nobody would know she was home. She was stuck at home, bored to death because we didn't have cable or internet. I had the doors double locked. I told her, when I came home, I would open the doors. I want to keep her safe.

When her mom came to pick her up, I told Nikki I would quit school and start working back in Indiana to take care of her and be with her.

She exclaimed, "No! You are finishing school."

She wanted me to go back with her so badly but she knew it was important for me to finish school so I could have a solid career. This beautiful girl has a heart that is unbelievable.

After her mom took her back to Indiana, I began feeling lonely. Nikki and I weren't always able to talk on the phone which destroyed my heart. I had nobody to talk to. I would come home after school and sit there contemplating if I should kill myself and end it all, but then I would focus on a picture of us from prom that was hanging on the wall. **This** made me smile and remember that she was carrying our child.

So I kept pushing on. I'm not going to lie and say I was a *man* and didn't cry. No, I was a man, and a human. I cried for my Nikki almost every day.

Quitting school was becoming more and more an option in my mind, but I knew Nikki would be disappointed. Back in Indiana she was living with her mom, aunt, and kids. I didn't want her in such a congested house so my parents helped out. They would take Nikki to our home were my sister and brother kept her company. I just wanted to be home with her.

In December, school was going on Christmas break so I decided, since my son was going to be born in a few months, I should take some time off from school. I went back home and took a four-month break to be with Nikki and watch my first child be born.

FATHERHOOD

The birth of Manuel, my firstborn son, opened my eyes and helped me to realize, this was all real. I was a father! Now I really had the important responsibility of making sure my family was well taken care of. I knew now, for sure, there was no more fun and games; it was time to grow up. I did mature, I can tell you that, but it wasn't fully and fast enough. There were times when I forgot I had the responsibilities of helping my wife around the house. By the way, I did say wife. Nikki and I got married a few days after our son was born.

To this day I am still trying to mature and better myself. After Manuel's birth and our union in Matrimony, we headed back to Pennsylvania, so I could finish school. It felt great to bring my little family along.

While I was in Indiana during Christmas break, I got a job at a place that had an office in Altoona, Pennsylvania. When we moved back, I asked for a transfer since the job was only 30 miles from my school. When I began working in Altoona it was completely different than what I had earlier experienced. The people were a little nicer to me. It didn't matter to them about race or the color of my skin.

However, now that I had my son, when we went to the store, people treated us worse than before because our baby was very light skinned. People saw I was with him and boy did they hate that. But it gave me something to be proud of. I figured they hated this, and instead of hiding, I'm going to prove to them we are good people. We ignored it so much, fewer people showed us their dirty looks, and just dealt with it because we weren't going anywhere yet.

Best of all, in May 2013 there was an addition to our family with the birth of Andru who was a little darker skinned than Manuel. Manuel was always a little helper with Andru who he loved to be around. Skipping slightly forward to August 2015, my wife and I welcomed Cruz, a special little girl who soften my heart so much. I didn't know this little girl would make me go crazy for her presence, because I began letting my macho man side go for my princess. At the age of 22 I had three gorgeous babies all close in age, and I knew they were my major life changing moments.

BACK TO INDIANA

In December 2012, I finished school with an Automotive Technician Custom Painting and Restoration Certification. We headed back to LaPorte and stayed with my parents for until we got our own place. It was a relief that my wife and I were moving up in life together and things were working out.

There were times people tried bullying me. They said things to me about my color of skin, my family being different colors than me, or my culture. I would defend my family first and foremost and educate anyone trying to say something about me.

Since seventh grade I had been writing lyrics and recording my rap-styled songs. And now I was becoming more and more eager to do music again. I had stopped for a long time while focusing on my family because my wife and I were trying to get a house. When we did get our house in nearby Michigan City, Indiana, the same town where my wife was from and where I worked in high school, we were ecstatic. We had something of ours that we worked hard for.

THE POWER OF APOLOGIZING

In 2014 I was working at an automotive dealership, an auto parts store, and a small car repair shop. One day when I was working at the auto parts store a guy who I had problems with in middle school came in. I greeted Zeth into my workplace and asked him how I could help. He started telling me what he needed and I had no problem helping him out. When he was leaving I told him I held no grudges against him from back in the day. He told me he was cool with me, and he's "not tripping over none of that."

That relieved me and made me feel comfortable. You see, even though I had problems with these guys, and I stopped doing what I did and kept my distance, I thought they would never forget what happened. I guess I was wrong.

In 2015, I was talking to Betty from Hey U.G.L.Y. about my music. I was shifting my lyric writing to send positive messages to people. I knew I was going to have to work my butt off since I had taken so many breaks from my music over the years. She thought it was a wonderful idea. I talked about it with my wife and asked her to help me along the way.

I had recorded a few new songs but I struggled because the pressures of everyday life depressing me. I posted the new music on social media and felt disappointed when people would just say it's good whether or not they really liked it. I found it helpful when people criticized my work and gave me suggestions on how I could improve. I delved more deeply into music because I wanted to help people who were suffering from the same things I had endured.

Betty had me on Hey U.G.L.Y.'s *Choose To Change* radio show, this time as an artist. After each of my songs played we talked about the lyrics and the importance of sharing them with the shows listeners worldwide. Just discussing the messages in my lyrics with her gave me the motivation to keep pushing.

Over lunch one day, Betty suggested I consider apologizing to anyone I had bullied. She explained how it could take a lot of pressure off my shoulders. I told her I had already apologized to one person and it did feel good. There were two more people, one of whom I was afraid to say anything to because old issues could get reopened. I told her I would apologize to these people anyway.

In the fall of 2015, I got on social media and messaged Aaron. He wasn't one of the people who bullied me, but was one I had bullied over some gang stuff. We would trash talk in public and almost got into a group fight at a local fair. I messaged him with fear in my mind and heart about what could happen.

The message was sent at 1:57pm October 25, 2015 : *Idk if you remember me. We went to school together. I was just messaging U to apologize for the difference we had back then. I have grown up n realized I did some dumb shit. Wanted to at least let u w.e beef we had back then has been long gone. N congrats on your family.*

He immediately got on and I saw these three little dots flickering meaning someone on the other end was typing. I was nervous, but then his message came through:

I remember you. Yeah everything is fine I never held no hate towards you. How you been bro?

I responded back.

That's good u doing good. N been alright. Living the adult life now u no

He said,

Lol, yea that I do know. Do you have family yourself?

I replied to him

Yea, I got 3 lil ones.

Him replying,

I try work hard n provide for my daughter n wife its great feeling having family...nice good job.

I finished off by saying

That's true it's a good feeling.

I was not expecting to hear any of this about 30 minutes before I messaged him, let alone a few years back. I felt even more relieved because things were finally coming off my shoulders. There was just one more person to apologize to but honestly, I was trying to avoid it as much as possible. Why? Well because this guy was Derek the kid who came looking for me at my house, the one who jumped me outside of my house, and the one who bullied me in school. I told Betty I was afraid of him because I still had the fear of, what if he tries to do something to me again. Now that I have a wife and kids, I need to protect them.

One day I got the courage to message Derek. My fingers were trembling because I didn't want to cause any more issues. But I knew this was the best way to get rid of the fear I carried within me.

On September 8, 2017 at 2:10pm I got on the social media app and messaged him privately saying:

Hey Derek do you remember me?

I waited because we weren't friends on social media so I had to see if he'd accept my request to view my message. I again saw those dots flickering like a strobe light on medium speed.
He replied back,

Yessir. What's up man. How you been bub?

I messaged back to him letting him know why I messaged him.

Not bad. I just wanted to hit u up n let u know that any differences we had in the past is past. Hope ur life is doing good bro.

He didn't respond. I worried that I had triggered some memories back into his head about all that had happened. I regretted messaging him because I felt stupid thinking he now definitely remembered me and would want to retaliate.

Well...I was completely wrong because on that same day at 3:33PM he replied back to me with a long message saying,

Bro I wasn't even upset about anything that happened before bub. That's all dead bro. We cool. I was gonna actually talk to you one day when I saw you at Automotive Center in La Porte but wasn't sure how cool you would've been so I didn't even bother bro. Lol. I've been decent tho. For the most part anyways.....

This made me feel relieved because I had held onto this fear in my chest and carried that pain for so, so long. Thinking that one day they would try to start things when I'm with my family, and it turned out to be, there was nothing. It was all squashed. Derek and I are mutual. We aren't best friends, but we have no problem if we pass each other. There was actually three times I saw him at the store and shook his hand saying it was good to see he is doing better in life.

TODAY

There were many things that happened to me that made me almost give up and end my life. As of this writing, summer of 2018, I can tell you things are a lot better. Yes, there are parts of life that I realize are always obstacles. Now I know that those obstacles are there to better ourselves. All the challenges I had throughout my life made me mentally stronger over time. During a few specific points when I thought I was never going to be able to get through it, I see that the struggle is what helped make me who I am today. I now laugh because I can't believe I made it through all of that.

1014 Photography

Today I am happily married to my best friend and have three smart and gorgeous children...my oldest son Manuel, next Andru and then, my daughter, Cruz. These kids kept, and continue to keep, giving me inspiration to continue in life because I want something amazing for them.

The other greatest person, who kept me going in life, and the reason why I stayed alive, is my high school sweetheart, my beautiful wife, Nikki. She stuck with me through some of the hardest times of my life and lived hard times with me. She experienced things she never thought she'd have to go through. She stuck by my side in the good and worst times of my life.

MY MUSIC

As you have read, life's challenges and all the other things needing my care, kept interrupting that important part of who I am.

Earlier in the book I told you I went by my *street nickname.* Today I go by **Lil Sylnc** (pronounced silence). I chose that name for many reasons. First, because of my personal silence during all of my pain and bullying. I wouldn't tell anybody about what happened to me. Second, because of my *no fists up* motto in combating societal ills, like bullying and racism. It takes a lot of strength to fight the good fight with words instead of fists. Third, I silence myself to hear others, so I can really listen to what's going on in order to be of help. Sometimes, when someone is struggling, all they need and want is a caring person to listen to what they have to say.

There is so much about me that people don't know and some of it can be understood through my music. I understand feelings and thoughts, so don't feel you are alone in life. The way you see me in my music is actually me; there is no other person. It is my feelings, my thoughts...it is me throughout it.

You can follow Lil Sylnc and my music on FaceBook, Twitter, Instagram, Reverb Nation, YouTube, and Bandcamp.

LESSONS LEARNED

One of the reasons I wrote this book was to help others kids who might be going through some of the same things I did. The other reason was to help parents, educators and other adults who don't see, or understand, the depth of pain that many kids can suffer. If I knew then, what I know now, I would have never suffered in silence. There are so many resources for students today, from school counselors to hotlines, where you can talk with or text experts, most of whom are survivors of the pain you are suffering. HeyUGLY.org has a great hotline list on their website that can help, whether you are suffering from being bullied, cutting or are suicidal. DO NOT keep all that pain bottled up inside of you. As you can see from my story, YOU are not alone.

I know it may seem hard to you now, but you've got to keep pushing through. Keep your head up. One day you will see the hard times become part of the past. I know people will try to bring you down and others will act like your friends and steer you down the wrong path, but you will have to be strong. I have left so many of my so-called friends behind, because my family is important and I chose to focus on them. I never know when the last day will be that I will be able to see my children. So, every day, I want to make sure I spend quality time cherishing them. My wife and kids might never know exactly how much they saved my life. I can tell you, being a father at a young age, for me, was well worth it because I changed for the better. I had to mature. I'm not saying for you to go out and get someone pregnant, or get pregnant at a young age, but just know, if it happens to you, don't feel trapped. People will say you are too young and put you down, but okay it's happening, you are in the process of having a baby, and it is now time to mature. There are things in my life I regret and wish I could turn back time, but I can't. I do know that, as crazy as it may seem, I wouldn't change a thing about what happened to me because if I did, I probably wouldn't be where I am today. I know I have purpose in my life and am a very happy man, husband, father, musician, and now, author.

Just like me, you have a purpose. My purpose is to help people with depression and suicidal thoughts. I'm creating a movement called, **Color The World**, to make all the shades of gray disappear and bring color (life or happiness) to the world, through my vlog, KYHU – Keep Your Head Up. As a proud member of Hey U.G.L.Y.'s Board of Directors and a survivor, it is important to me to help out the kids in school who are suicidal, being abused, and/or being bullied.

You can help me in my quest to save lives. If you know someone who is in pain, you can help keep them alive by just listening. You will know if they want your advice or opinion.

And lastly, I learned to become a better father and husband. I haven't fully matured yet because I can still be self-centered at times. I can tell you that I look at myself now and see a totally different person. That doesn't mean I'm done changing for the better, no not at all, but I see more progress in my life. There are times I still get depressed, but now I can look at those times and be like, *I will be okay. I know so*. I keep my head up and look at my family, my joys of life.

ACKNOWLEDGMENTS

I want to thank a few people in my life who made me who I am today, helped me with this book and kept me alive:

Nikki, who continues to be there for me, and always does her hardest to help. My wonderful kids for giving me something to work hard for. *Mi jefita, jefe,* sister, and brother, for helping me out as I got older, even though I shut them out in my middle and high school years.

Betty Hoeffner from Hey U.G.L.Y. (Unique Gifted Lovable You); she showed me so many paths I can take with my life and helped me hold my head up higher than what I thought I could.

Mrs. V for helping me out with scholarship opportunities and starting me on the right path to a better life and the officer I met in middle school who tried setting me straight. Even though I didn't listen to him right away, I later reflected on life and realized, if he wouldn't have had that talk with me, I would have continued down that bad road.

Special thanks to Arnie Saks for helping to shape and edit this book with Betty and myself over those many, many weeks.

Al Baker for his help in designing the cover and website for my book. Dalia Vitkus for her diligent final edits.

I want to thank all the people who took the chance to read this book and hope it opened your mind a little to realize you are important, your life is precious, you have a purpose, and so much more. You are one of the reasons why I continue with my music and try to help people. I am "Lil Sylnc" (silence) from MidWest Homie's Recordz, here to Color The World. Shhhh!

REFERENCES

www.heyugly.org

www. ProjectApologize.org

www.AlmostBulliedToDeath.com

lilsylnc.weebly.com

facebook.com/lilsylnc

twitter.com/lilsylnc

instagram.com/lilsylnc

reverbnation.com/lilsylnc

bandcamp.com/lilsylnc

To schedule Victor Vargas for a book signing, or to speak at your next event, email AlmostBulliedToDeath@gmail.com

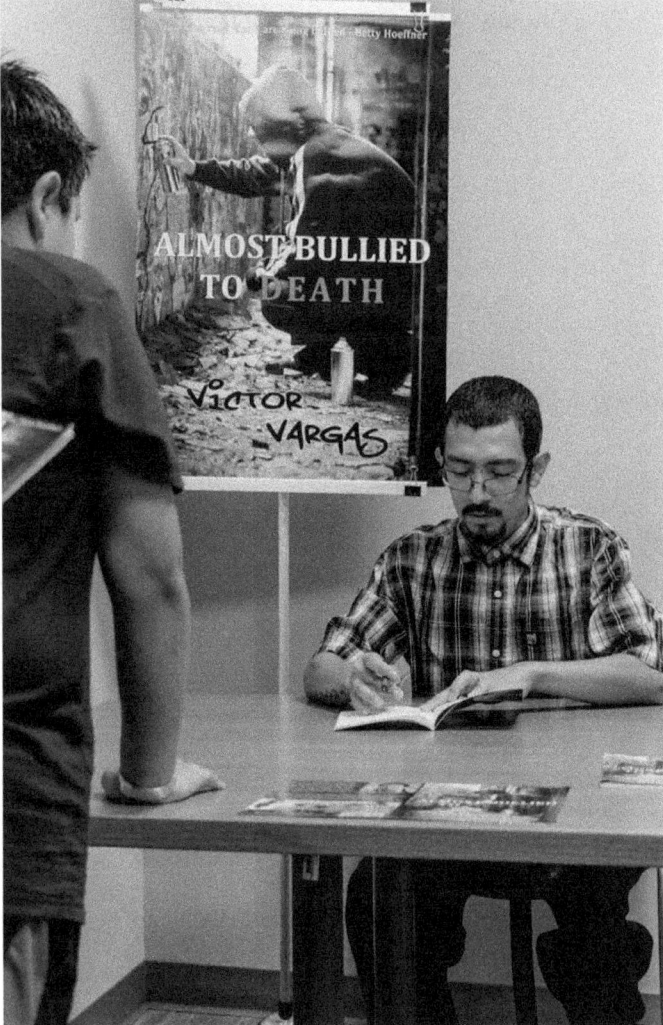

Eddy Bibian Photography

www.ingramcontent.com/pod-product-compliance
Lightning Source LLC
Chambersburg PA
CBHW062010040426
42447CB00010B/1989